When We
See Ourselves

Black x Brown Love

Jonah Batambuze
Arsheen Shamaila

Foreword by: Rene Caryol MBE

We have tremendous gratitude for the team and for the people who joined us on this journey.

Jonah Batambuze and Swetha Maddula-Batambuze

#BlindianProject

When We See Ourselves
Black x Brown Love

Published by Jonah Batambuze / #BlindianProject Publishing
ISBN 978-1-5272-9072-3

Design by: SeyPEG
Cover Design: Sukruti Anah Staneley

#WhenWeSeeOurselves
www.blindian-project.com

ALL LIVES
CAN'T MATTER
UNTIL #BLACK
LIVES MATTER
MADE IN CHINA
KGS

If you're reading this, you've survived 2020 — a year which will arguably go down as a defining moment in history. As our lives were unexpectedly thrown into a tailspin by the global COVID-19 pandemic, our values were tested. We were also forced to confront racial inequalities tearing at humanity's threads.

Amidst the chaos, Black x Brown communities found themselves disproportionately affected by the pandemic and systemic racism. However, instead of allowing the turmoil to divide our communities further, this moment brought these groups closer together.

Black x Brown relationships are an inevitable feature and reality wherever the two communities coexist. These relationships are often plagued by stories of racism, classism, and Anti-Blackness — rather than celebrated. *Until now.*

Inspired by a racial uprising, not witnessed since the 1960s Civil Rights Movement, When We See Ourselves is a collection of intimate short stories, reflections, and artwork providing a first-person account of Black x Brown love. These love stories allow us to reflect on stereotypes and biases within our lives and ultimately, help create a better world.

Jonah Batambuze

FOREWORD BY:
RENE CARAYOL MBE
London, U.K.

This is an important and hopeful book which captures the rapidly and positively changing times when it comes to race. We live in an incredibly cosmopolitan world, but it doesn't always feel that way for everyone. There are still far too many dangerous divides, and too many people who are still sheltering in over segregated areas and mindsets.

Jonah has the energy, drive and the cause - all bottled into his young body and mind - to make this book a vital part of the way forward for all of us who are already part of the Black and Indian partnership dynamic.

From the moment Jonah and I met, it was impossible to ignore his natural enthusiasm and goodwill to all of humanity. He has this inherent ability to lock into the good he sees in everyone, no matter what their background or shortcomings. We all need a "Jonah" in our lives.

Social justice has marched into all of our lives, demanding our attention, from so many different angles; The Me Too and Black Lives Matter movements and hate crimes against Asians, amongst many. This book is needed now more than ever. There are so many myths, so many great and positive stories that need sharing and the not so great experiences that need sharing too. This all needs doing in a balanced and sensitive manner, but most of all, they need telling.

As with most of the best stories, they come alive from those with the "lived experience", those who have actually "walked in the shoes" and those who have tasted the joy of mixed relationships and the riches of shared heritage and cultures.

When Jonah joined myself and some members of my team on a Zoom call, it soon became clear that all of us had first-hand experience of Black and Asian relationships. We all smiled and instantly started finishing off each other's sentences. We laughed and shared each other's pain and frustrations.

Jonah is a force of nature. He is beautifully positioned to be the curator and narrator of this really important book. This book may not have worked 5 years ago. It is still a little ahead of its time, but it will now have a significant impact and following. It gives me great pleasure and is a huge privilege to write this introduction.

I welcome you all to a growing and fabulous intersection of the most vibrant and important cultures.

No Place Like London

When we initially started seeing each other, I hadn't realized just how tough it might be for her, in terms of the issues she would face because I was Black. She never made a big issue of it, but every now and again, it would really get to her. She was born in Chandigarh and had come to London when she was 10 years old.

There was a big family wedding coming up and she was a bit apprehensive about the whole affair, I could tell, but she didn't want to talk about it. The Mehndi night was approaching, a celebration before the wedding, just for the bride and her female friends. It's where they have the beautiful henna designs put on their hands and feet.

She left and I could sense things were a little fraught. I soon realised it was the first, big family gathering since we had been together. I could sense that she was dead nervous and anxious about how her relatives might react.

It didn't take long before her fears were proved correct. One of her older aunts came right over and commented, "You look happy and have a new spring in your step – have you met someone new?"

She was a little taken aback, but smiled and responded, "Well in actual fact, I have met someone."

Her aunt smiled back and said, "I'm so happy for you, do we know him?"

"No."

Her aunt was now intrigued, "Is he a local? Is he Indian?"

She smiled again and answered, "No."

Her aunt was clearly surprised and said, "Is he British, white then?"

She shook her head.

Her aunt now was looking very worried and had her hands by her head, "He's not Muslim?" she asked
in a disbelieving voice.

Again, she shook her head.

Her aunt was now clearly lost. She then looked up and said, "No, he's not Black, is he?"

With a disappointing sigh, she said, "Yes."

Her aunt looked aghast, and then just walked away.

They were standing and talking on a slightly elevated stage. As she backed off in complete shock, she tripped and fell off the stage. Fortunately, she wasn't at all hurt but her ego had been badly bruised. It felt a lot like karma. My partner rushed over, helped her up and steadied her.

She was fine and instantly said to her, "That was God paying me back for being so cruel to you. I'm so sorry for behaving like that. I'm very pleased for you. If you're happy, I'm happy for you too."

I received an immediate text with a full update on what had just happened. I now better understood what she was having to go through. We spoke about it a lot later that night. She was having to be very strong, and it was so tough. It was very hard to dress this up as anything other than abject racism. I'm very pleased that she has had no issues at all with any of my friends or family.

That night in particular, the genie of race could not go back in the bottle. The generational divide had been laid bare in front of her. Inclusion is a mindset and an attitude. It's beyond words but language does matter, and it's the attitude behind the language that matters most.
The future belongs to those brave enough to change it together.

Rene Carayol MBE

Jonah Batambuze

After spending the last 12 years of my life married to the game of basketball, in 2001, I jumped at a once-in-a-lifetime opportunity to study abroad in Dublin, Ireland. Little did I know, God planned for me to meet an Indian princess who would change my life forever.

What were the chances of our paths randomly crossing? I was a first-generation Ugandan-American who only attended UCD for a semester. While I'd spent my entire life eating samosas, I had never shared an intimate conversation with an Indian person. Swetha briefly lived in Ireland following her family's move from Guntur, Andhra Pradesh, and was visiting a childhood friend who lived in the same dormitory.

Our gazes met while cooking dinner in the boisterous communal kitchens. Later that night, we connected at a local pub, appropriately named "The Mad Hatter." A spark was lit.

At the end of the semester, I went back to the States. A few months passed, and we met in Chicago while Swetha attended a family wedding. Call me naïve, but I was hoping to meet some of her friends and family while picking her up from the hotel's reception. We met around the corner. Back then, I was ignorant of how the community would gossip if anyone saw us leaving together.

Swetha Maddula-Batambuze

After a night on the town dancing to R&B, Hip Hop and Reggae — we decided to make things official. Sure, there were thousands of miles between us but I don't think either one of us cared. It felt right.

Swetha met my parents relatively early in our relationship. They loved her from the beginning. Having lived alongside South Asians in Uganda, their only concern was whether I'd be accepted by Swetha's extended family and community.

As things progressed, I wondered when she would introduce me to her parents and started dropping hints. It felt like she was waiting for the perfect timing. Not knowing the culture, I had no idea what telling her parents meant.

Another year passed before Swetha was able to mention me to her parents. Her mother stumbled across a photo of mine on her computer. Several questions followed on who I was, but for the most part — her parents tried to avoid the conversation. I think they hoped the relationship would blow over. It never did.

My now brother-in-law and several aunties and uncles were the first members of Swetha's family I met. They advocated for our relationship and the latter convinced my now in-laws to meet me.

I'll never forget our first meeting... "What are your intentions for our daughter?" my now father-in-law asked once the initial pleasantries were out of the way. "We want to get married." I responded, knowing there was only one response to his question. That first meeting wasn't easy, but it was one of the many steps of the process.

I'd be lying if I said that doubt never crept into my mind along our journey. I often felt vulnerable and exposed, as if our relationship could abruptly end. And the fact that none of my friends could relate made the situation even more isolating. But, I couldn't dismiss how this love made me feel. Every day, Swetha challenges me to be a better person, and for that, I'm grateful.

As I reminisce on moments of our lives, I thank Swetha for always believing in our love. Her strength never exhibited how difficult it was.

If I could go back in time, I'd remind myself that Swetha wasn't your average girl from the Midwest. And, regardless of me not being Indian, not being from the same caste, or studying medicine — our love would inspire thousands of Black x Brown people worldwide to unite in the form of the #BlindianProject.

● **Swetha**

As the parents of two mixed-race children, we must help them feel comfortable in their skin.

"We don't celebrate Eid; she's never had home cooked biryani."

Mishka

Kyah and I met at the beginning of the national COVID-19 lockdown in April 2020, following my breakup. We both swiped right on each other. She was the first Brown woman to ever swipe right on me. I hadn't had much interaction with Brown women at that point. I was aware of colorism and racism within the community, so I wasn't surprised to have never matched with anyone from that community.

I was nervous about re-entering the dating scene in general, regardless of race, as I was a newly single mother to a precocious toddler and hadn't been on a date with someone new in almost seven years!

After a few weeks of speaking and meeting up for socially distanced walks in parks, I wanted to see where things could go. I had initially thought that race would play a large role in our relationship. Still, it became apparent very quickly that Kyah's emotional generosity and warmth were far more important to me than the difference in our races. Perhaps meeting during the lockdown focused our attention on each other more keenly. We have faced challenges with co-parenting with my ex-partner and acknowledging and addressing previous relationships' poor habits. Kyah is teaching me that true

partnership only exists with true equality in the relationship. She also continues to teach me the importance of holding space for myself with compassion and patience.

Encountering and navigating Kyah's Pakistani heritage hasn't been something that I've had to do much. After coming out to her family, she no longer has a relationship with them. I've had no experience attending family or religious events. I know that losing that community brings Kyah sorrow.

Kyah has been very proactive in learning about my Jamaican culture and my experience as a Black British lesbian. It's been refreshing to view it through Kyah's eyes and see my place anew in this world as a queer black woman.

Being on a journey with her has been the most unexpected and amazing chapter of my life. I can't wait to see what beautiful tapestry we weave together with the combined richness of our cultures and experiences.

Mishka

Ultimately my relationship with Kyah, although visibly marked by our races, brings much more complexity and joy to my life than just this difference.

Kyah

I grew up in a British-Pakistani family. I didn't know I was gay. I only knew that as I aged and became more aware of my world, I became unhappy and despairing for reasons I didn't understand. I knew that I hated the idea of marrying a "culturally permissible" man; I knew that I couldn't imagine being happy with anyone my parents liked. As a 12 year-old, I didn't know why.

I felt intellectually at odds with a lot of the "truths" I was being told. I also didn't understand why my outspokenness or questioning the "truths" was considered so awful. My father was often angry about things that I didn't see as particularly dramatic to be upset about - that I made a new friend at a debating tournament who was a boy, that I wore a skirt to play hockey, that I got a B. I thought the tensions of our cultural gulfs were the reason I felt so depressed all the time.

Despite numerous "obvious" indications through my youth, I didn't consider the possibility that I was gay. That was also a consequence of the times. Between a section 28 adhering school, limited representation of LGBTQ persons on the media (let alone South Asian ones), and growing up in a Muslim home, I didn't know anything about gay people.

When I did start having a clue, I immediately went into a remarkably fierce state of denial. That must have been self-preservation. I struggled to cope with the truth in my 20s, let alone as a child and teenager. I still can't be sure what was worse - the "inexplicable," chronic depression that set in from age 12 or the full weight of the truth, which I admitted to myself at age 24.

There were a lot of international boarding student at my school—many from African families. Save fo a few key exceptions; I didn't "fit in" with my whit peers. I felt more cultural similarity with my Africa peers. Equal parental pressure and expectation, the similarly confusing context of immense familia love and laughter (or at least, what I understoo immense familial love to be - my definition is no different).

My family and the Desi community made me fee special and loved but selectively and conditionally I felt caught between wars. Warring parents, wh were an ill-fitting arranged marriage match; th war in myself, between my truth and my want fo tribe/connection. I also felt incredibly overwhelm ing guilt and shame. I felt personally responsibl for bringing my parents sadness and that it was m duty to put myself aside for them.

It took a long time to understand and reject th "truths" and the cruelty of the emotional blackmai ing and manipulation that runs rife. It's not right t "live through your children." It's not right to lov them on the condition they do what you want ther to. It's not right to close your mind to understand ing and learning. It's not right to view your child a someone you own - and can therefore disown.

Sadly, many are merely modeling the parentin they had and saw. It takes bravery to stand u to the community pressure - about having a ga child, or a Black son or daughter-in-law. Or any thing else that 'breaks the mould.' It takes braver to question the "truths" you've been taught abou God. Parents are just people, and some peopl aren't brave.

I no longer have a relationship with my family or the Desi community. I've gained a lot of joy and sanity and happiness from forming a tribe elsewhere. A resolution hasn't been possible. This story needs to be told as much as the ones where love has trumped prejudice.

I haven't had to navigate any fall out from having a black partner because of the fall out already from being gay. My wonderful partner Mishka is Jamaican. She doesn't have a lot of understanding of my cultural background. We don't celebrate Eid; she's never had home cooked biryani (mine is rubbish!). She hasn't picked up any Urdu from events. She doesn't know the difference between the various religious customs. She's never been to a crazy full-on Desi wedding. She's never been force-fed by an auntie, and then told she looks moti *(chubby)*.

But she's also never had to deal with the anti-blackness in the community either. Or the homophobia. Maybe that's worth the losses.

I hope anyone reading this who is not LGBTQIA and is involved in the South Asian/Muslim community remembers that LGBTQIA Desis need your allyship. Speak loudly and positively about us to the aunties and uncles you know, post about Pride, talk about LGBTQIA friends. You never know which kid in the corner is listening.

● **Kyah**

As all good love stories do, our love story begins with how we each came to love ourselves enough to walk the paths that lead us here.

IN THE

DMs

The love stories you share have been a blessing and gotten me through these lockdowns. But recently, there was a post you shared with a gay couple that disturbed me. It's a known fact that Europeans and Americans spread homosexuality amongst our communities.

problem   problem   problem
Please don't become a part of the **problem.**   problem
                                problem   problem
                            problem

problem   10:34
                            problem
    problem

        problem

Queerness is present in various cultures around the world going back centuries. For you to say that Europeans and Americans are responsible for spreading homosexuality is 100% unequivocally incorrect. The #BlindianProject is an LGBTQ+ safe space and will continue to be so indefinitely.

11:23

Share a(n) (un)conscious bias you have regarding queer people.

_____
_____
_____
_____
_____
_____
_____
_____
_____
_____
_____
_____

Type Message…

BEING
INTER
RELATION
DOESN'T
I
LOVE
CULT

IN AN

RACIAL

SHIP

MEAN

DONT

MY

URE

Michelene & Farhan

We met in our early 20s through mutual friends on Cinco De Mayo. As Farhan casually strolled into the Mexican restaurant after a night of celebration, it was like a breath of fresh air. Instead of your standard greeting, I opted for,

"Wow, You're gorgeous!" to which he responded with equal enthusiasm, "Wow, you have a beautiful smile!"

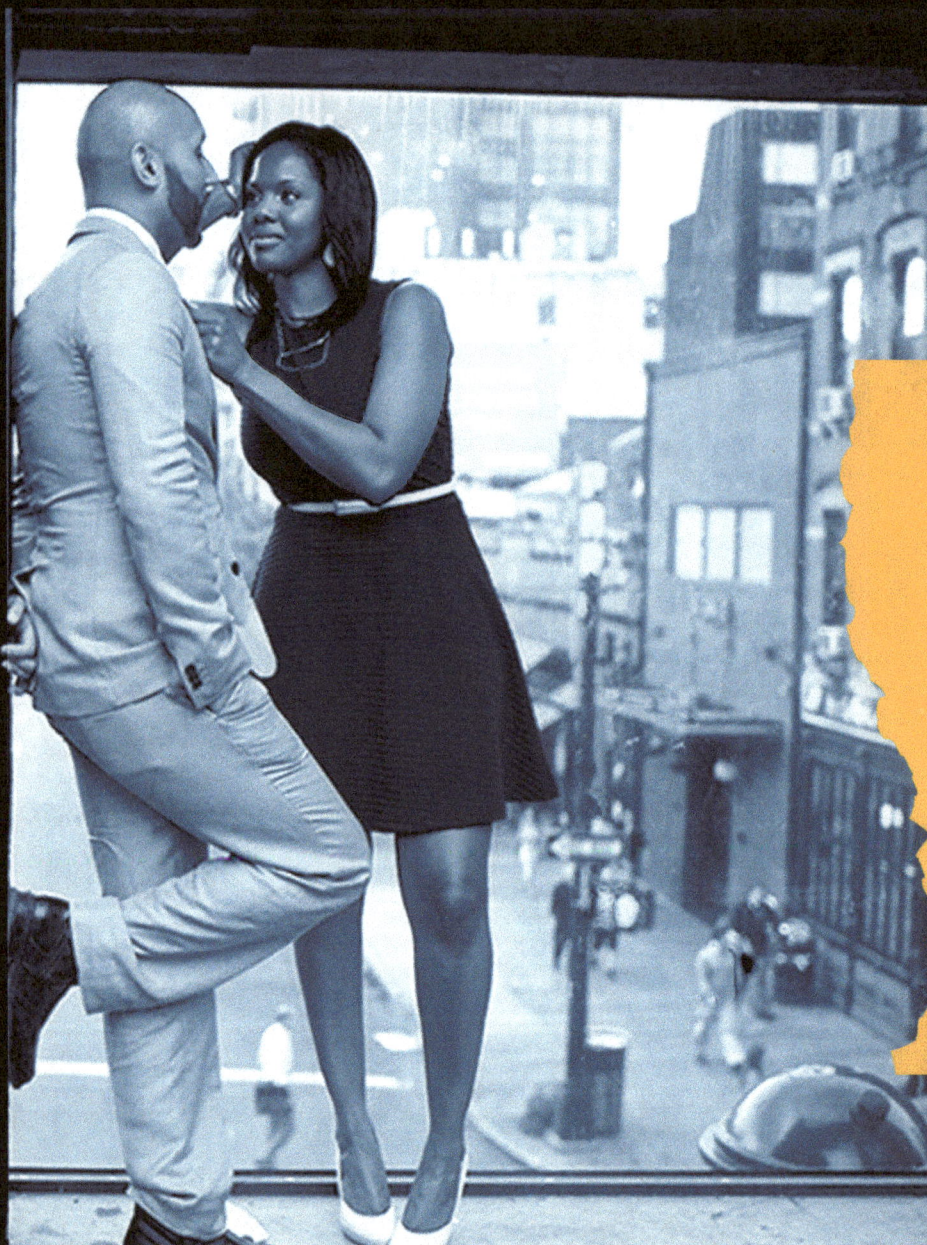

THE ONE

Farhan is a first-genera Pakistani-American. He born in Jersey City, after parents and older brother migrated from Pakistan. I African-American, born in N York City. My father is f North Carolina and my mo is from Long Island.

Before Farhan, I had er dated anyone outside Black community before. time it was different thoug knew he was the "one" a the first date.

In the most loving tone, my mom once said to me, "I want you to know that a lot of people might not see it the way you do. People don't see love the way you do."

I had no idea what she meant. I blew my breath and with a defensive attitude, I said, "Please, everyone is going to love us."

The truth is, society doesn't know how to look at us. I see Black men staring at me with disappointment, while Black women ask me, "Does he have a brother?"

My brother had done two tours in the Middle East and felt Muslim men didn't respect women. He made me promise that I would tell him if my husband ever hit me. Like, pinky swear promise. I couldn't believe we were having that discussion but he was seriously concerned about my safety.

Despite Farhan being Muslim, he never asked me to convert. He was even okay with me keeping my last name. But, I was naïve to think that Farhan was as open as I was. I didn't live my life in secrets, Farhan did. It didn't hit me until Farhan told me I couldn't attend his med school graduation because his parents were going to be there. That's when I understood what my mom meant.

As we stood at the altar, with no one but my family, he promised that "our love will warm the coldest of hearts."

Well, it's been almost 13 years, and I've never met his mother - or anyone in his family. I couldn't even attend his father's funeral. Farhan's parents aren't overly religious. Ironically, his mother loves the Obamas — especially Michelle. I've come to realize that Farhan's parents are old school and his mother had a plan for her son. I wasn't in the plan.

During these times, I make a selfless decision to put his family first. I believe a mother should have a healthy relationship with her son. I think she should come first. I believe it's important for him to love her without distraction. I encourage it. All of this comes from my own relationship with my mother - and it helps me understand the bigger picture.

Either way, the pain is real for the both of us.

But we both know our love has a greater purpose - and we know we wouldn't fully appreciate the deepness of our love without experiencing the pain. Our love story isn't perfect but our love story is real.

This is us.

● Michelene

At first, I didn't understand how painful the rejection would be. As I'm getting older, I feel it more. It has forced my husband to live a second life. I feel like he hasn't fought hard enough for us. He feels like he gave up everything for us. This will always be a work in progress.

IN THE DMs

I'm in my first interracial relationship. We both fought so hard to get to where we are. However, I feel guilty for the negativity my partner has experienced because of our relationship. He is the most considerate person and is intentional about helping out his community. Sometimes I feel he's a target for being taken advantage of because is so generous

When we've been out together, I've heard people openly refer to my partner as a sell-out. How do I handle this?

15:

It's normal to feel guilty that your relationship has contributed to some of the negativity your partner has experienced. This is not to say that you're doing anything wrong, because clearly — you're not. You have to realize that some people have been conditioned to believe that dating/marrying interracially is turning your back on your culture — which obviously isn't the case.

16:02

Recall a time you were called out for turning your back on your culture, and describe how it made you feel.

_____
_____
_____
_____
_____
_____
_____
_____
_____
_____
_____
_____

Type Message…

"Honestly, there weren't any big adjustments made to my life other than prayer, and not eating pork."

Wayne and I met in Spanish class in high school when I was 15 years old. The teacher asked us to describe each other. Wayne said that I was beautiful. I responded by saying that he was ugly. I guess that extraordinary things start in unique ways.

Ruksana Carroll

To say that we're different is an understatement. I'm a 4'4 South Indian Muslim girl, and Wayne is a 6'1 African-American Christian boy with roots from New Jersey, North and South Carolina. We quickly became best friends and fell in love amidst our friendship.

Our families shared the same core values. From day one, Wayne's family treated me like family. There was an initial shock at first sight, but that quickly wore off as my personality revealed itself.

My parents and immediate family have always been very open-minded. As my height differentiated me from most, I never thought they'd have an issue with me marrying someone of another race or religion. They judged people purely on their character and were aware of Wayne and my longstanding friendship.

There was never an issue with Wayne's religious beliefs, but parents being parents — they did ask him what his thoughts on conversion were. Wayne grew up Christian Baptist, but wasn't really into religion growing up.

Wayne was familiar with Islam through his friends. Although he converted for me, Islam brought him a lot of peace and offered him healing after the death of his mother.

In 2012, we got married and have a beautiful daughter named Yaara. She is five years old and is truly the best of both worlds. She's been the light of our family, and through her, my parents' heart and smiles couldn't have been bigger!

My parents raised me to fight for what I believe in. Fortunately, they trusted me when I told them I found the perfect match! But, I always think that one must stay true to themselves and the people they love — believing that God has a plan for you. No one can change your fate, and if your family doesn't agree to It, be the first to pave the way and make a change!

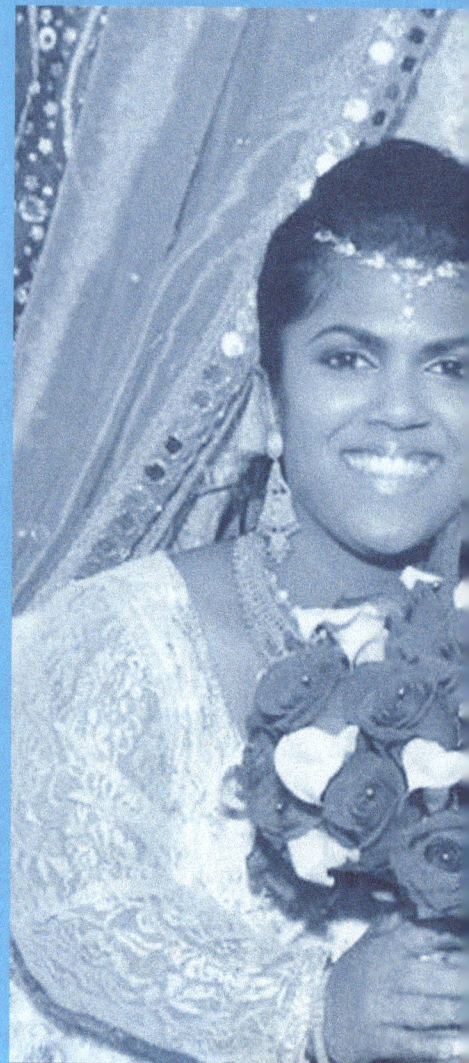

Wanye Carroll Jr.

Right from the gate, you can tell Ruksana and I are different. Not only physically, but ethnically. And to be honest, I believe that's one of the reasons why we work so well. Opposites attract, right? Well, these opposites definitely did attract, and I'm glad that the universe brought her into my life.

My parents and immediate family have always been very supportive of anything and everything I've ever done. In 2012, when we decided to get married, there was the matter of religious beliefs and background. Which, for the record, her parents had no issue with. But just so that there would be no issues whatsoever with our union in the eyes of Allah, converting to Islam was my last step in making this legit.

For me, converting to Islam was easy. I've always been aware of Islam via best friends and family. The practices and values of Islam were not foreign to me and I've always embraced them. Honestly, there weren't any big adjustments made to my life other than prayer, and not eating pork.

For some reason or another, after taking my Shahada (Muslim declaration of faith), it made me feel whole. Especially in a time when I was dealing with the loss of my mother, I literally felt at peace with anything and everything going in my life at that time. And I still do.

IN THE DMs

I'm a massive fan of your page, and reading the stories you share gives me hope and strength for the future of Browns and Blacks to merge. However, I have one concern. Please try to understand where I am coming from.

Stories about South Asian Muslim and Black couples have been focusing a bit too much on "conversion" to Islam. That's great if that works for you; however, that is not a fair representation of many other South Asians who aren't Muslim.

Could you suggest that people who want to share their story focus less on the "conversion component" and focus more on how their parents accepted a **Black** partner for them?

Or, how about not mentioning it at all? Your page isn't just catering to South Asian Muslims and Blacks. Many South Asians like myself are not able to connect to conversion stories because they only relate to South Asian Muslims.

13:13

Thank you for reaching out. We take great integrity in the stories we decide to publish. While I appreciate your comments, alongside anti-Blackness, Islamophobia is another prejudice in our communities that needs to be fought. We believe in having difficult conversations. So, erasing what may be a significant part of our stories because they make some people uncomfortable isn't something we believe in. We are all capable of learning from these stories and challenging our beliefs.

14:26

IN THE DMs

**What three prejudices do you carry about Islam?
How can we work towards ending Islamophobia?**

_____

_____

_____

_____

_____

_____

_____

_____

_____

_____

_____

Type Message…

"Most people in my family had never dealt with a deaf person and didn't know how to communicate with me. I was ignored. I was left

out."

Kasmira Patel & Derrick Butler

In South Asian culture, it's common to be mistreated and ignored if you're disabled. I was born deaf and grew up using ASL as my primary form of communication. When I wasn't with my parents, I spent my time alone. Most people in my family had never dealt with a deaf person and didn't know how to communicate with me. I was ignored. I was left out.

Thus, it was important for me to find a life partner who was knowledgeable about deaf culture and able to communicate with me.

Derrick is African-American and Indigenous. He was born with partial hearing and learned ASL in elementary school. Derrick grew up in a Christian household, where he was taught that faith, prayer, and having a relationship with God are several of life's important virtues. He was also taught that everyone is created equally and with the blood under God's image.

We met in the cafeteria at Rochester Institute of Technology, which has a mixed population of hearing and deaf students. Derrick walked over to me, introduced himself, and then told me I was the most beautiful girl in the world.

We became friends, started hanging out, and quickly became close. I never thought I would fall in love with Derrick. Meanwhile, my parents were on the lookout for an Indian partner. Arranged marriages were all my parents knew. When they found several matches for me that didn't know sign language, there was an obvious communication barrier. My parents began to understand my needs in a partner.

When I told my parents about Derrick, they were shocked because he wasn't Indian. The reactions and judgments have differed amongst family members. Eventually, my parents put my needs first, which made it easier for me to communicate with them. We received their blessings and got married two years ago.

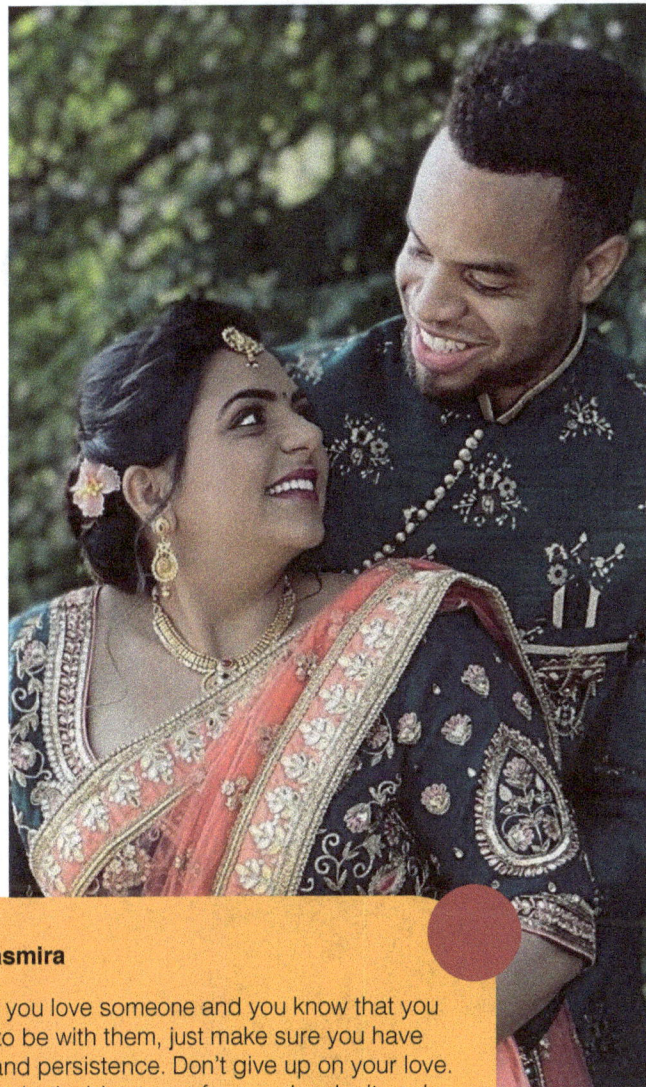

● **Kasmira**

When you love someone and you know that you want to be with them, just make sure you have faith and persistence. Don't give up on your love. It takes both sides to conform and make it work.

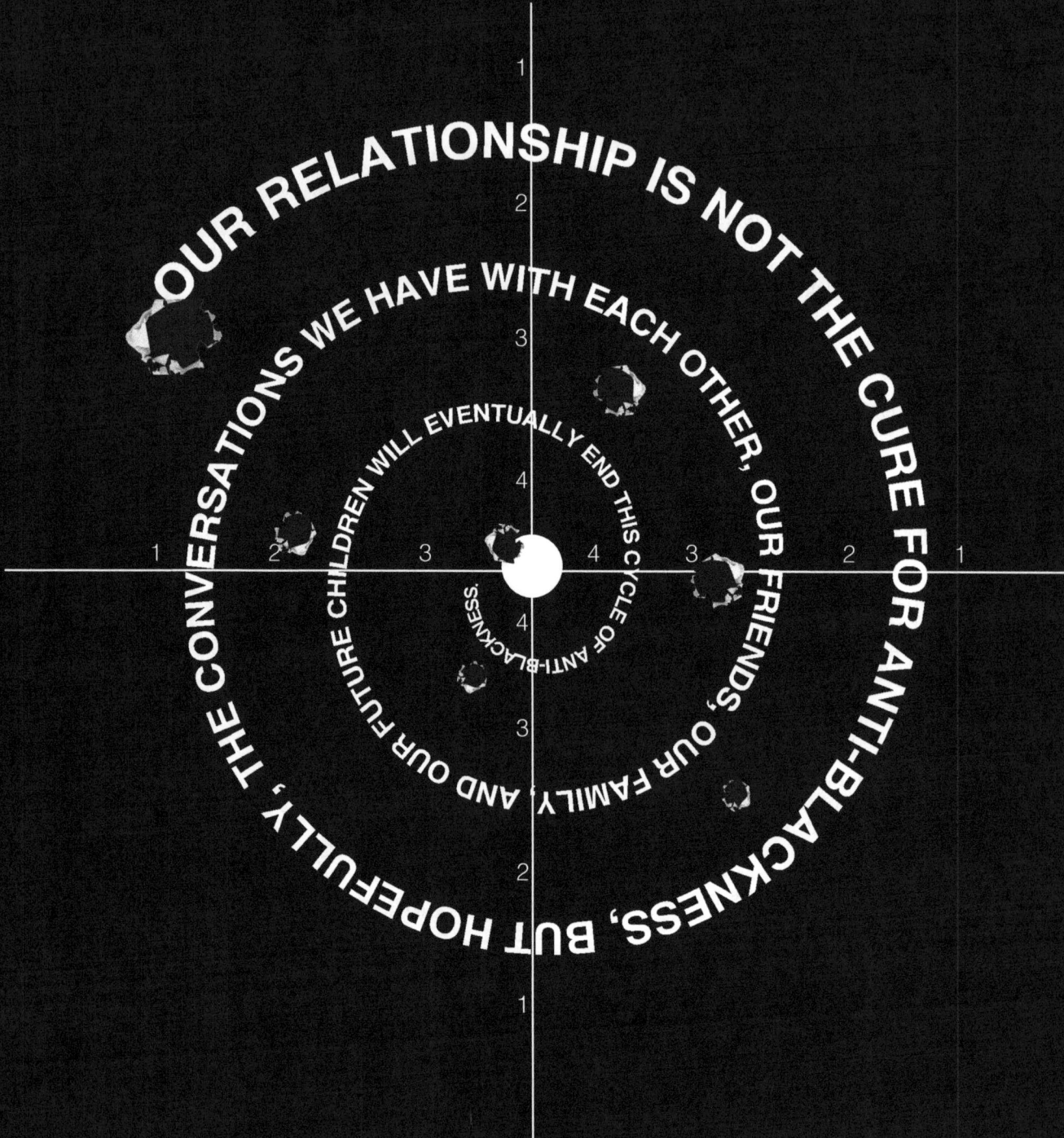

OUR RELATIONSHIP IS NOT THE CURE FOR ANTI-BLACKNESS, BUT HOPEFULLY, THE CONVERSATIONS WE HAVE WITH EACH OTHER, OUR FRIENDS, OUR FAMILY, AND OUR FUTURE CHILDREN WILL EVENTUALLY END THIS CYCLE OF ANTI-BLACKNESS.

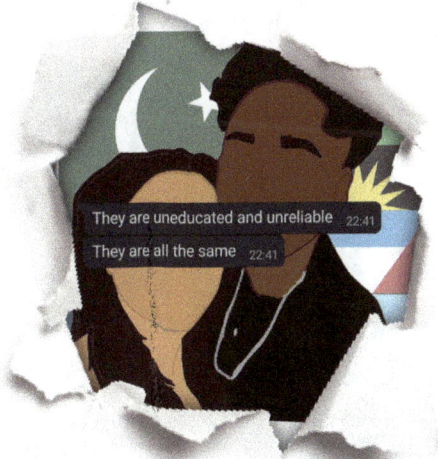

Angelica Razack-Francis & John Francis

As I reflect on my "love life" or lack thereof before John, I thought I was undesirable.

No one found me attractive (White, Brown, etc.) except for Black men. I'd often say, "Only Black guys are into me." As if I was cursed or doomed. Looking back, I came to the uncomfortable realization that my dating preferences were anti-Black. And while anti-Black- ness is something that is learned, I still can either perpetuate this sentiment, or challenge and unlearn it.

THIS IS US.

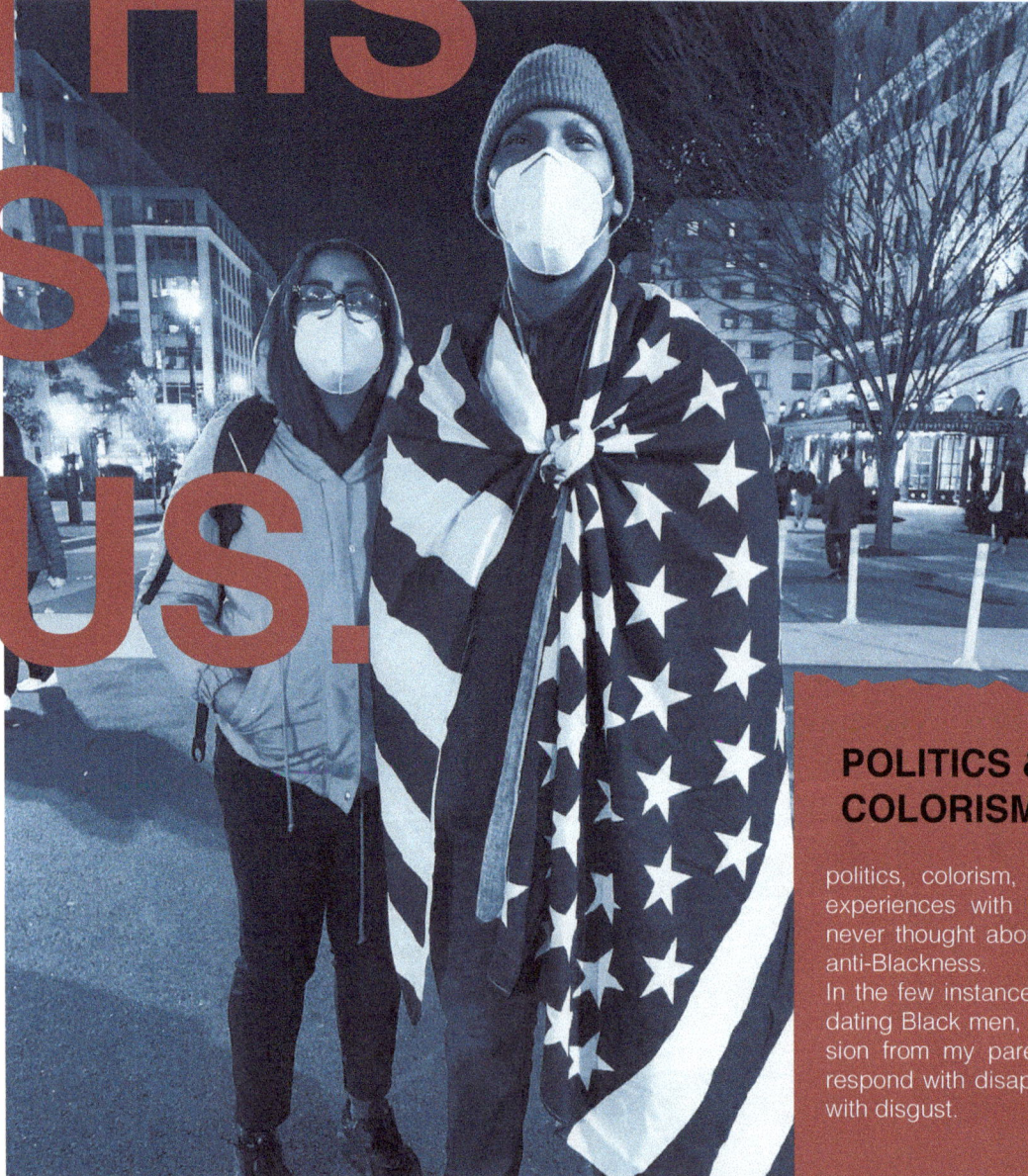

There was a period my life that I chose perpetuate it. I active sought out Indo-Ca ibbean or South Asi men throughout my 2 because I wanted please my Guyane parents. My family Indo-Caribbean, a they preferred to s me with a South Asi or Indo-Caribbean ma Also, in Guyana, the Inc an people look down the Black people. Ho ever, I never thoug about challenging r parents' anti-Blacknes

POLITICS & COLORISM

politics, colorism, and my family's personal experiences with Black people. However, I never thought about challenging my parents' anti-Blackness.
In the few instances that I showed interest in dating Black men, I felt that I needed permis- sion from my parents. But my father would respond with disappointment, and my mother with disgust.

Then there was John. We met in law school, and for some reason, he was attracted to my arrogant law school gunner energy. I remember him approaching another classmate and me while we were studying, and he casually sat down and started talking to us. I honestly found him annoying, but somehow we ended up going to a panel discussion that night. We talked about Dragon Ball Z and other anime on the subway and missed our stop three or four times. I remember thinking to myself, "What is this?" But I dismissed those thoughts because even if we became more than friends, my parents would disapprove. However, after two years of friendship and me challenging my anti-Blackness — I chose happiness.

My parents weren't happy with my decision and didn't want to meet John in the first few months of our relationship. I firmly stood my ground, and my sister told my parents to be more supportive. Once they gave John a chance, they loved him.

We are currently engaged. Our relationship is not the cure for anti-Blackness, but hopefully, the conversations we have with each other, our friends, our family, and our future children will eventually end this cycle of anti-Blackness.

Angelica

While anti-Blackness is something that is learned, still can either perpetuate his sentiment, or challenge and unlearn it.

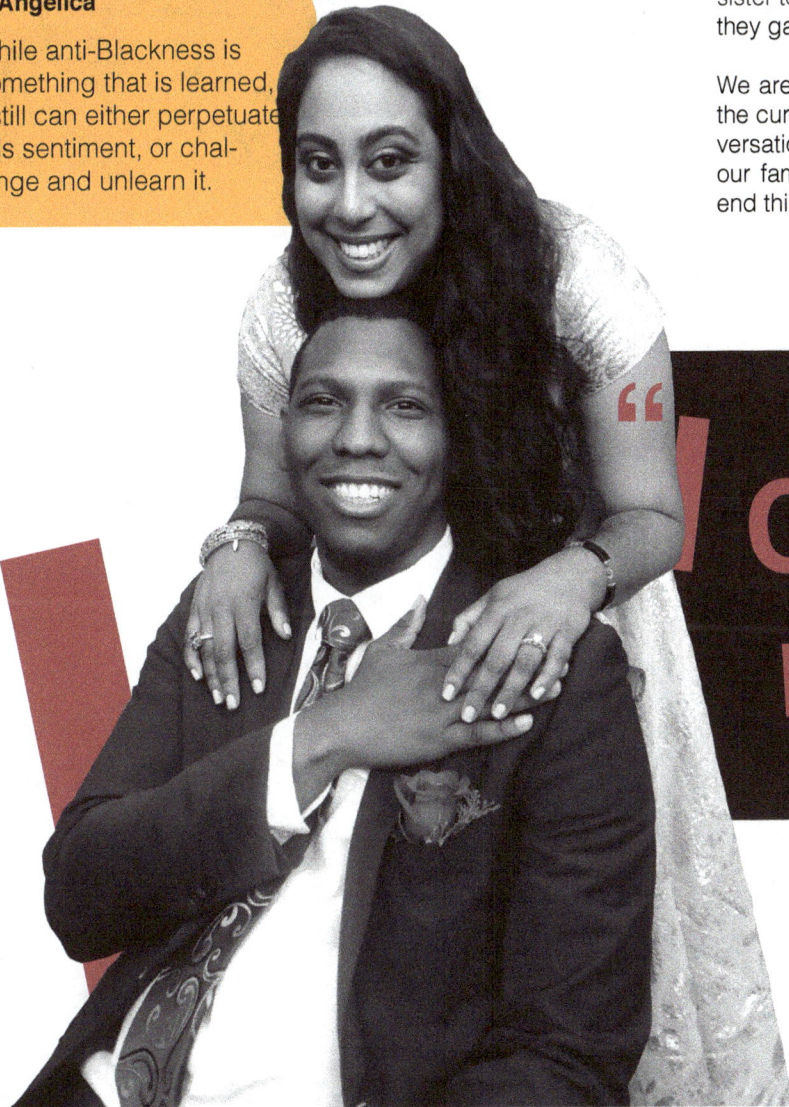

"I CHOSE HAPPINESS."

IN THE
DMS

I am so sick and tired of everything being about BLM. Watching some of these media outlets, the only people you would think are getting killed by the police are Blacks.

You never see the unjustified police brutality, etc. against Whites, Asians, and Indians. I wonder why?

06:33

You've missed the point entirely. This isn't a popularity contest; instead, it is a life and death situation for Black people.

If the concept of BLM makes you feel uncomfortable, then you should ask yourself why. The idea of Black Lives Matter doesn't detract or diminish your experiences or achievements. Instead, Black Lives Matter acknowledges an issue staring us in the face that needs to be addressed. Supporting others in need with a helping hand should never be frowned upon.

09:16

IN THE DMs

What are some traits of anti-Blackness that you experience in your daily life and how can you challenge those views?

Type Message...

"SOMEDAY I'LL MEET THAT PERSON

THAT I'LL MAKE A BIRYANI X JOLLOF RICE

FUSION DISH WITH.

BUT IN THIS MOMENT,

I SMILE,

BECAUSE I'M HAPPY TO BE

WHERE I AM NOW."

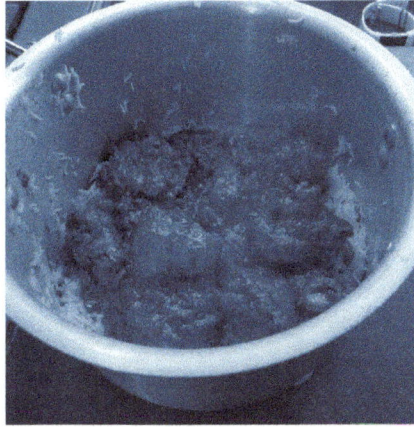

Vincent

I was born in Port Harcourt, Nigeria. I'm the eldest of five children and the only son. My family left Nigeria for the USA when I was three, and later, we moved to Johannesburg, South Africa, when I was eight. As a third culture kid, my cultural identity is fluid. I speak with a blended accent that highlights the different places I've lived.

My father is a professor, and my mother is a researcher. They come from two different areas of Nigeria and represent two of the country's distinct cultures. My father is Ikwere, and my mother is Yoruba.

My mother raised us to do our best and leave the rest in God's hands. My father's outlook was that we should all abide by his rules. We were taught that we needed to achieve more than others in the community — or risk disgracing the family.

As I grew older, I connected closely with Desi folks because of our surprising similarities. My immediate circle of close friends was mostly Desi. Both of our communities contained stories of aunties and uncles who "came to this country with a dollar in their pockets."

Through my connection to Desi folks, I understood certain aspects of my life better. My father wasn't impressed. "Do you have no pride in yourself as a person?" he asked. He claimed that I was trying to be someone I wasn't and losing myself to another inherently foreign culture.

We met on Valentine's Day. Cliché, I know, but her smile had me in a puddle. I know it's not the manliest thing to say, but there was something about her that put me at peace. We both wrote poetry and sometimes would share our work. It wasn't overly romantic, merely a window into the other person's feelings.

The first time I met her mother was at an event held on campus. Her daughter was beaming and introduced me as her friend. Her mother had this look of shock, horror, and confusion on her face. I think, in part, to the excitement in which her daughter introduced me.

You can only imagine my father's response when I told him about a Desi woman I was interested in pursuing. He reminded me of all the sacrifices he had made for the family. He asked, "How could you betray the family like this?"

Essentially, I would be painting a poor image of the family within the community, even though none of my father's matchmaking efforts progressed past the point of a quick laugh from my father's friends.

My father had a tremendous attachment to his village. He mentioned what the family would say about a foreign woman who wasn't dedicated to the village (note neither my mother nor my sisters have the dedication my father wishes us to have for his village).

"The children that would result from such a union would not know who they are," my father exclaimed. Did I mention, I'm my parent's only son? The oldest child. I am the person responsible for carrying on my father's legacy. The cultural expectations were suffocating. Had I forgotten my duty and obligations to the family?

In a nutshell, there was drama. She was also disgracing the family being seen with a Black man. She was also reminded of her duty to the family.

We spoke about the things that were happening on both fronts. Over time, some of the comments reduced. Officially, we were no longer friends. Her sister knew that we were still talking and would sometimes go for drives together — while avoiding anyone who knew either of us. I blocked out my father's commentary altogether, and we decided to work on us.

It didn't last. Things had taken a toll on her mental health, and her mother wanted her to marry ASAP. She was 26-years-old, after all, and her younger sister had found someone.

After several months, things finally fizzled out. Later, I learned that she'd returned home and married. I was happy for her and wished her the best. I knew she'd wanted to settle down.

Being with her has contributed to the man I am today and the person I will be in the future. I'm grateful for all of it. I grew up. I upgraded my fashion sense. I set boundaries between the cultural expectations put on me. I evolved and continue to grow. I don't think we appreciate the amount of growth we can gain even when things don't work out.

To some, interracial relationships mean a betrayal to your own. Especially in South Africa, a country where there are still some racial tensions between different ethnic groups. But I'm optimistic that things will get there someday.

Someday I'll meet that person that I'll find a way to make a biryani x jollof rice fusion dish with. But in this moment, I smile, because I'm happy to be where I am now.

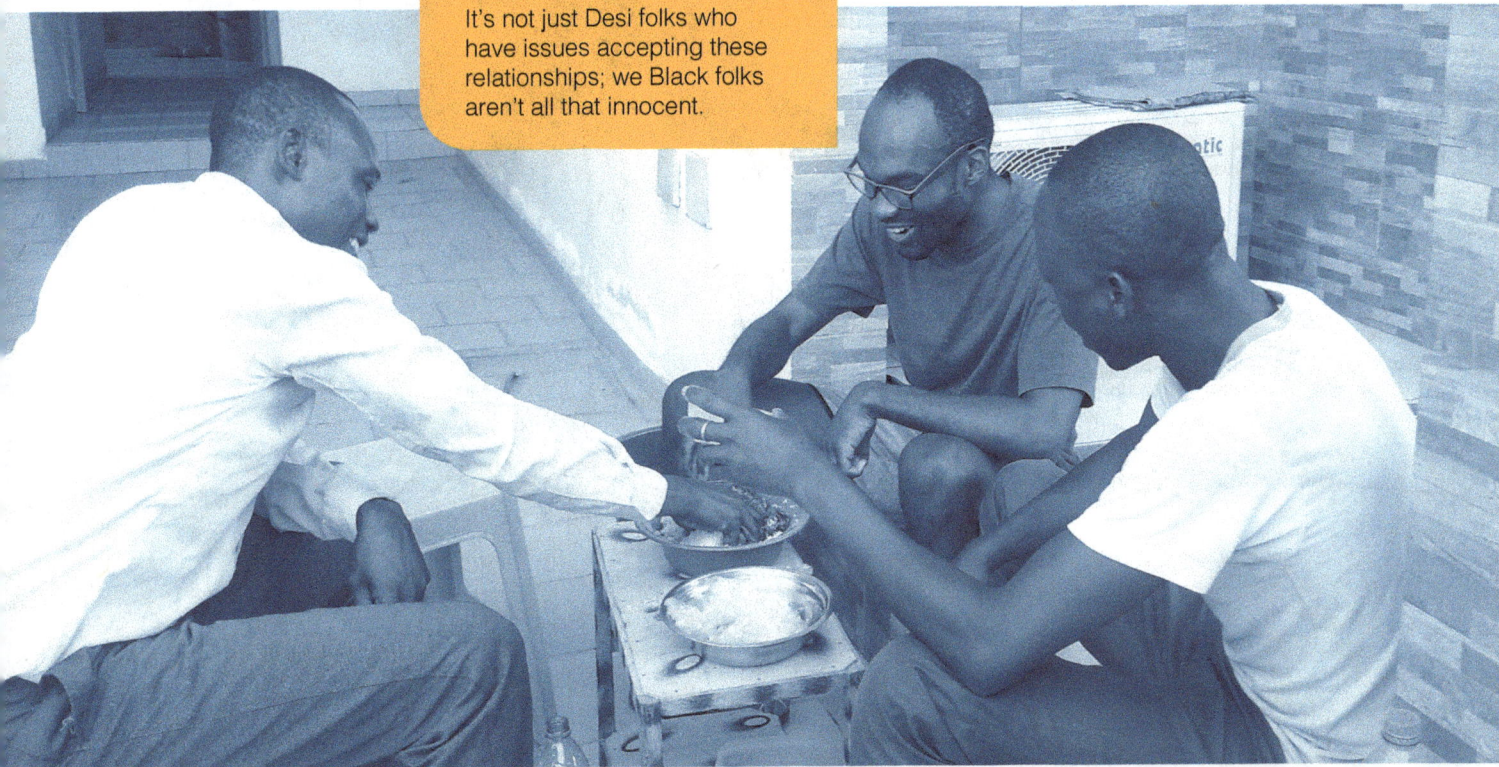

● **Vincent**

It's not just Desi folks who have issues accepting these relationships; we Black folks aren't all that innocent.

IN THE DMs

I'm tired of Asians coming into Black communities.

The only reason they are here is to take our money.
They don't reinvest in our communities.
They look down upon us.

Why should the Black community be interested
in solidarity with this community?

11:38

The term "model minority" was coined in 1966 by sociologist William Peterson in an article written for the NY Times magazine. Shortly after the publication, many other outlets ran similar success stories of Asian-American groups.

They don't want us to unite.

Imagine how powerful we'd be if we found commonalities between our experiences and united against our "real" enemy.

15:21

What stereotypes do we hold about "model minority" communities? What can we do to dismantle the "model minority" myth?

_____
_____
_____
_____
_____
_____
_____
_____
_____
_____
_____
_____

Type Message…

BEING LIGHT-SKINNED DOESN'T INVALIDATE THE EXPERIENCES OF SELF-IDENTIFYING PEOPLE OF COLOR.

Natasha Piette & Shawn Basheer

I met Shawn seven years ago. Oddly, immediately after meeting, I added him to all social media platforms, even LinkedIn. I couldn't help his quirky, yet familiar sense of humour, cute geekiness, ability to eat finger foods at the same pace as me, and his Bollywood prince-look stuck with me. He's a Malayali first-generation British-Muslim. I'm a mixed Bissau-Guinean, Lebanese, British American Baha'i'.

" **You never know what course of smaller, seemingly insignificant life events will lead to a lifetime of love.**

For those not familiar, the Baha'i faith's central tenets are the oneness of religion, the unity of races, the equality of women and men and the harmony of science and religion.

We met at an event to commemorate the Arms Trade Treaty's ratification as part of a recognized group of Amnesty International UK student activists. Neither of us were meant to be at the event, however, our other activist friends couldn't attend.

When we filed for our marriage certificate in New Hampshire, the only options to mark were White or Black. I refused to choose one over the other, as it would be a denial of a part of me. But we couldn't receive the marriage certificate without selecting a race.

I'm aware that my skin color affords me privileges. I'm also aware that I'm Black and proud to be Black. No one can ever take that away from me, no matter what their assumptions are about me. I am who I am.

Some extended family on both sides have been quick to judge. We've faced Islamophobia, with members of my family asking if I'd be forcefully converted, whether I'd have to cover up now that I'm married to a Muslim, and also asking what Shawn's thoughts are on 9/11. Luckily, the younger generations of my family step in each time, or I usually try to counter their assumptions.

Whereas on the Indian side of this marriage, anti-Blackness manifests itself in generalizing the African experience and not recognizing it as a diverse continent. There've also been off-hand remarks about the fairness of skin equating to beauty. I always wonder about how accommodating they would be if I wasn't as light-skinned as I am.

We've had to counter their preconceptions and show them love, while protecting ourselves from that kind of negative energy. We are especially aware of this now, as we're expecting a little one and want them to embrace their Blindian heritage.

My husband is my best friend and the most wonderful human being on the planet. Our love for social justice, a mutual love of food, and our outright silliness are just a few qualities of our partnership that I treasure. Sometimes, you never know what course of smaller, seemingly insignificant life events will lead to a lifetime of love.

● **Natasha**

The registrar casually told me that she'd put me down as White and moved on quickly to the next sections of the registration. I was left stunned and felt deeply uncomfortable, as if who I am had been erased.

IN THE DMs

Sometimes it feels as if biracial people can pick and choose what race they want to suit their needs. Take Kamala Harris, who only recently started identifying as South Asian publicly, for what I assume are votes.

Please HELP me understand how she gets to use whatever pass she wants?

No one, and I mean no one, should ever try and police a mixed-race person on what/how they should identify. In Kamala Harris' case, she's received double discrimination. One minute she's too Black, the next she's not Black enough. The same could be said about her South Asian identity. There is so much suspicion and the need to put Harris in a box but, ultimately, it's the individual's decision on how they identify.

Think of a time that you misidentified someone's race. What stereotypes had you formed about that person based on your assumption?

_____
_____
_____
_____
_____
_____
_____
_____
_____
_____
_____
_____
_____

Type Message…

Lost

Love

I wish there was a platform like the Blindian Project all those years ago because it would've given me the hope I was searching for at the time.

The Modern Couple

I first met Ike when I was in first year of university through a mutual friend. Whenever we saw each other, it was an exchange of pleasantries at most rather than anything more.

I was in my final year at University when I bumped into him again, only this time it was different - I noticed something I never had before. He was sweet, funny and kind – not to mention handsome! We continued speaking and then began to date.

I could relax around him and be my goofy self. We just got each other. If it were an American movie, he would be the popular footballer, whereas I would've been the studious, lowkey type. Despite our differences, I felt like the luckiest woman in the world.

I was honest with him from day one about my parents and the likelihood of them not accepting him. I wanted to give him a chance to walk away. To my surprise, his response was soothing and he assured me he understood the ramifications of being together. Despite all that, he still wanted to be with me.

We were dating for the best part of a year when I decided to tell my parents about him. I was tired of lying, and honestly wanted to live my life in peace - to build foundation with the man I loved but it wasn't that simple.

I was living at home after university and the secrecy began to eat away at me, as well as the geographical distance between Ike and I. So I told them. I thought I was ready but nothing could've prepared me for the words I heard next.

My parents told me that they would disown me if I continued to "go down that path". It was clear that they didn't care about me, or what Ike was like as a person – because they just saw him as a Black Man. It was a cycle of emotional abuse as well as feeling isolated in my own home. I felt like a shell of my former self and decided it was best to end it with Ike. Not because I didn't want to be with him but because he ended up being the only happy thing in my life at the time.

Fast forward five months later, we reconnected and it felt like nothing had changed between him and I. The spark was still there. At that point, I realized I had to live life for myself and not for the expectations my parents and my community had of me.

I continued to keep the relationship a secret with the guise that Ike was a friend. I introduced him as a friend to my parents. They met him a few times and to their credit kept an open mind, until I finally told them we were together. It was a struggle, but after years of pushing they came around to accepting him. It wasn't perfect by any means but it was a relief.

I was lucky in the sense Ike's family accepted me from the moment he introduced me, which was such a lovely contrast to what he had inadvertently experienced on the flip side. Whilst Ike and I are no longer together, I'm proud that throughout this journey, I've remained true to myself. I've learned so much and taken many gifts from my relationship with Ike. I've understood more about mental health, red flags in relationships, boundaries and most importantly, healing.

Since then, I've spent years writing and welcomed the birth of The Modern Couple. I want to share my story hoping that it could help support others who've experienced something similar, even if it's just one person; for love has no color.

IN THE DMs

Things haven't been great since I told my parents about my relationship. For the last three months, been walking on eggshells, scared to do anything wrong in fear that an argument will break out. I ha en't had a proper conversation with my parents s and my mental health is deteriorating.

How can I make our situation better?

I'm sorry you're in this situation. If you and your partner are serious, I often think that counseling with a person aware of the cultural nuances at play can do wonders for your relationship and situation. If the relationship is something that you believe in, you need to find the courage to speak with your parents, letting them know how you feel.

22:45

IN THE DMs

What are three lessons you've learned from a past relationship?

_____
_____
_____
_____
_____
_____
_____
_____
_____
_____
_____
_____

Type Message…

"As a child, I was fed a diet of Martin Luther King and Malcolm X, and an understanding that I would be stereotyped in a very particular way, through the lens of anti-Black stereotypes and tropes."

Banseka Kayembe

"Your grandfather never approved of our marriage." This sentence was cautiously delivered to me by my Indian mother over lunch, as we sat together at the dining table when I was 17 years old. I wasn't expecting us to be having a particularly serious conversation and in many ways it was a piece of information I didn't really know what to do with. I asked a few questions but my memory is hazy. Like the remnants of my meal, I swallowed the knowledge quietly; I gave it relatively little thought for a long time.

For many Indians reading this, you may have already guessed why my parent's relationship didn't have my mother's father's approval. My mother's siblings married white people, which was seen as bearable to him, if less than ideal. However, my dad being Black was deemed as too much of a taboo; something unacceptable. The reasons are inescapably bigoted of course, rooted in a deep sense of anti-Blackness and a delusional view of Black people as culturally and possibly even biologically inferior.

I never really thought much about my mother's father at all, which seems odd knowing what I know now. I knew, as a Sikh man, he had been a survivor of the partition, making the haunting journey from the Punjab, Pakistan to India. He immigrated to the UK in the 1960s, with my grandmother and their children. He died when I was five years old and I have no memories of him.

His presence in my life was always lingering in the background, barely registering with me. Perhaps there'd be a faded photograph of him sitting on a mantelpiece, vague childhood memories of the garden he'd tended to at my grandparent's old bungalow in Hastings, or my grandma mentioning him with a wry smile whilst she dished out an unmistakably English dinner of fish fingers, egg and chips after school. I was probably more concerned with the food than old stories from the past.

My dad is Congolese, and Blackness is most commonly how I've been seen and understood. My mother is smart and knew that although her children came from two heritages, our practical reality was one of Blackness, especially giv we were growing up in the UK. I was f a diet of Martin Luther King and Malco X, and an understanding that I would stereotyped in a very particular wa through the lens of anti-Black stere types and tropes.

I've explored my heritage within the la couple of years, which in turn has forc me to reckon with the deep anti-Blac ness that still exists within Indian co munities. It's always going to be diffic to see yourself as part of a heritage th on some level is also trying to reje you. It's an uncomfortable paradox. I' faced awkward moments with British- dians, confused and unsure how to spond when my heritage has come u a vague nod of acknowledgement cc pled with widened eyes, with no foll up questions.

The 2020 Black Lives Matter moveme brought into sharper focus how troub some these issues are, helping to bri me back full circle. issues are, helpi to bring me back full circle. Much I

happy with identifying predominant-
as Black. Personally I've never felt
ot Black enough" for Black people
though I'm not being dismissive of
ers who do) and in contrast to almost
y other group, I've always felt a sense
unconditional acceptance within the
mmunity.

ese issues are much bigger than just
nily fallouts and fragments of person-
stories. For many Indians, a period of
lection, both of yourself, your com-
inity and the structures you inhabit
nains vital. You must recognise that
doing nothing, you play your part in
holding White supremacy, a system
ich sees Black people at the bottom,
d ironically oppresses people of color
well.

alse belief in Indians being part of a
odel minority" is delusional, but in the
g run also deeply harmful to your-
ves; certainly in the UK. The move-
ent for Black civil rights in the 1950s
d 60s oversaw huge benefits for Indi-
s living here too. It also doesn't make
you to be cheering on a Black wom-

an of South Asian heritage in the White
House, whilst refusing to condemn exist-
ing anti-Black taboos and stereotypes.

My family history is just, sort of there,
lingering like the memories of my mother's father. There's nothing I can do to
change it. Historical traumas of these
actions don't disappear, but live on
through the younger generations. Perhaps if enough people from the Indian
community take action, it'll be less com-
plicated for others.

IN THE DMs

Your page is an embarrassment and is sickening to the development of Brown people. Your page is effectively displaying the harsh truth of this movement, and that is Black guys mainly banging cheap Brown girls who are embarrassed by their own culture.

Most of the pictures are of Black men with Brown girls, very rarely the other way around. Because the harsh truth is, most Black people are not attractive, and cheap Brown girls have all brought into this "it's cool to be Black. I want to get banged out by Blacks. Or, I want to show off that I'm with a Black guy." This is the same for White people. Most White girls getting banged out by Black guys because they're cheap and easy.

I feel sorry for you that you believe Black men are to blame for your issues. Firstly, I can't imagine that you know any of the women on this page. So, for you to insinuate that they're cheap, shows a deeper issue with self-confidence on your part.

You're the reason why Brown kids find it difficult to integrate and be popular amongst girls because you show Black guys are more popular.

22:42

SECONDLY, BE BETTER.

People like you are the reason why communities like the #BlindianProject exist.

23:36

Describe ways in which society hypersexualizes Black men.

_____
_____
_____
_____
_____
_____
_____
_____
_____
_____
_____
_____
_____

Type Message…

i try to emulate light in darkness
lead with love even if hate is their language
lead with strength even when submission is their guidance
try to translate their thoughts into my deepest passages

roses out of concrete, magic
unlearning the hate,
embracing the love, magic

Capitalize our identities.
don't capitalize on them.
because
the weight of my identity demands attention.
take notice.

- Arsheen Shamaila

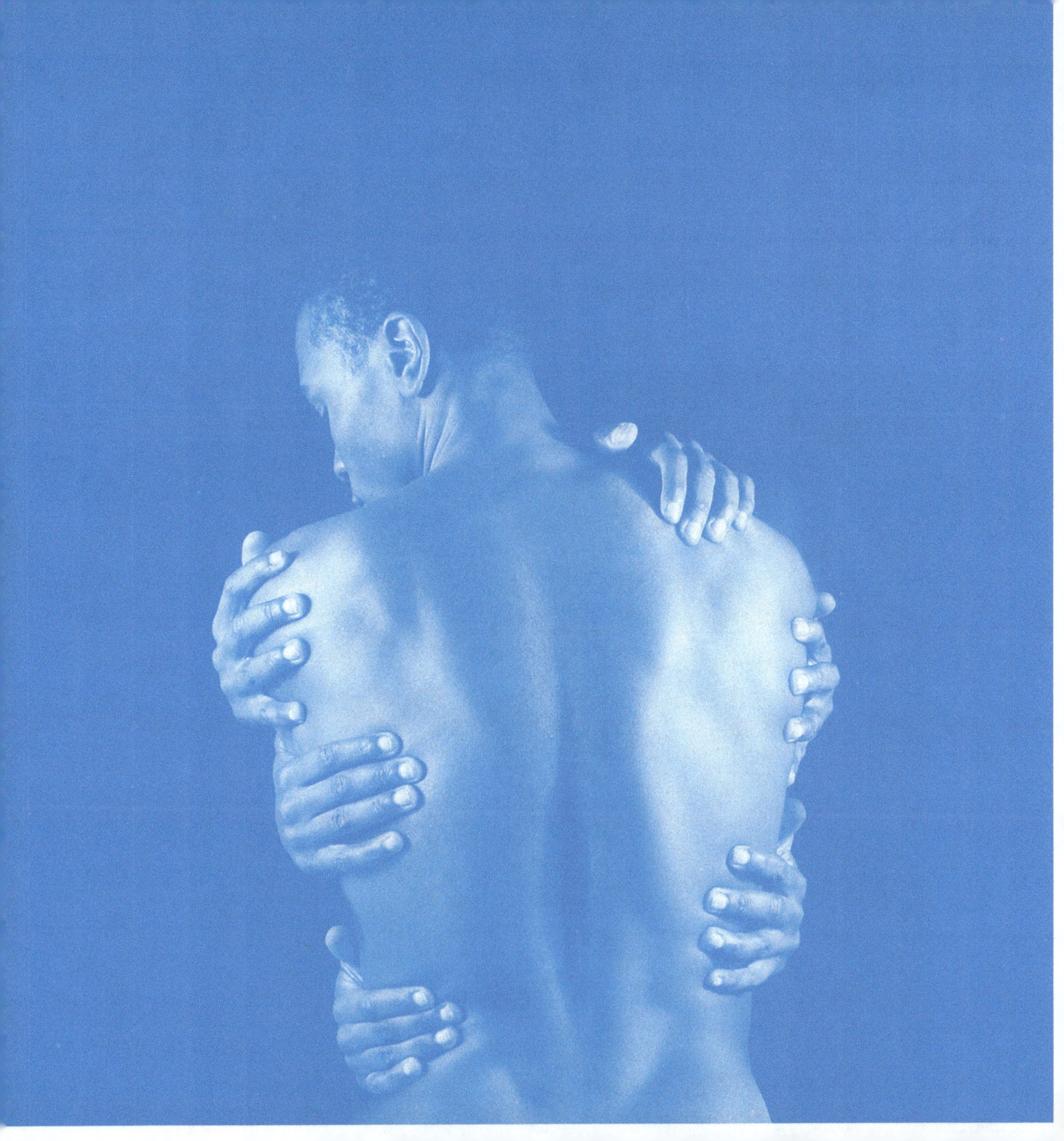

Taneesha Hill

Karen

Sana

Rini Rejin

Karen Xavier

Priti

Swetha Maddula Batambuze

Grace Kulubya

C

Priti Patel

Iyla Joy Batambuze

Franc

Ajani Jagan Batam

Priti Thakkar

Ephraim Winston

Jyoti Iyer

Anita Shah

Jacqueline Lara

Dipti Patel

Caroline Batambuze

Suman Maddula

Marcel Plummer

Marcel Plummer

Alonza Mitchell

Meenam Rastogi

Priya Santokhee

Gomar Charlton

Un

Auntie Dhurga

Manu Chawla

Bhavika Panchal

Charles Earl

Avnash Vird

Anusha Mathew

Rini Rejinold

Mar

Raphael Harry

Deepa Coston

Neena

Danny Cadet

Jose Olasa

Upside Down Smilie

Ronica Rupa

Hima Veeramachaneni

Danny Cadet

Shani Wijemur

Vincent Obisie-Oriu

Ricky St Claire

Natasha P. Basheer

Samiya Brasfield

Ash Bibi

otte Kagale Batambuze

Indi Moseti

alima Kulubya

Louise Campbell

Gurkeert Bagri

Sam Lamptey

Andrew Mondragon

uze

Tim James

Seyi Ajewole

Lipika Bhan

Batambuze

Arsheen Shamaila

Ayesha Syeddah

anohar Maddula

Dilpreet Kaur

ha Kiron Konda

Dipali Limbachia

Sam

Abrham & Keert

Humaira Chuhan

Zarmeena Waseem

Baljit Badyal

Priya Nandhra

Anjali Gowda Ferguson

Sharan Sanghera

BN Kumar

Sapna Vadgama

on Hill

Jiwan Dhaliwal

Bhavika Panchal

anjana Murthy

Nina Bhalla

Neelima Nadella

Zain Haider

Chanelle Peterson

Ruksana Carroll

Annie H

Andrae Goldson

Hetal Naik

Sushmita Banda

How to Introduce Your Partner to Your Parents

101

A crash course on achieving what is likely one of the most challenging parts of our relationships.

Get Cultured

Take an active interest in learning about your partner's culture
- Eat the food
- Read the stories
- Dance to the music
- Experience the religion
- Wear the clothes

Challenge anti-Blackness

There is nothing wrong with challenging anti-Blackness in those closest to you. Once you understand what's shaped your loved one's perceptions, it's much easier to dismantle them. With many racial issues brought to the forefront, this is the best time to have these conversations.

Check your relationship

Don't be surprised if asked, "What are your intentions for our son/daughter?" at the first meeting. Check your relationship and ask yourself whether this is a life partnership. The last thing you want to do is be unclear in your head and still questioning what you want. Do the work in advance.

Discuss the future

The sooner you and your partner start having meaningful discussions about how you'll live your lives and raise your family, the better. You may find out that your lives aren't compatible. However, it's better to know these things before an expensive wedding.

When will we start building a family?
What kind of parenting style will we adapt?
What religion will we raise the children with?

Find Allies within the community

Often, there are family members or aunties and/or uncles within the community that your parents will go to for guidance. Start identifying these people and building relationships with them. Share your love story, bring them into the fold, and help them showcase your love. You'll be surprised how far a recommendation from an auntie or uncle can go in your favor.

Don't be discouraged

This is a process. Dismantling internal biases requires frequent conversations and attempts to change your loved one's perceptive. You'll have moments of success and moments of hurt. Try not to get discouraged and continue forward.

an a date

ggling the expectations of family, along-
e your partner is no easy feat. No one likes
feel left in the dark. Have conversations
nongst yourselves regarding when you'd
nt the introduction to happen and form a
an.

Be Mentally Prepared

The reality is that we can be disowned for choosing to love outside our cultures. Throughout the process, we'll likely hear racist and negative stereotypes. Stay focused on the goal and take time to self-educate about the deeply rooted cultural biases that contribute to these reactions. Think optimistically, but plan pessimistically.

Support each other

Getting through this process isn't easy. Remember that you and your partner are in this fight together. If you're struggling to have meaningful conversations amongst yourselves, a counselor or finding people with similar experiences will be helpful.

Be Yourself

Remember that your partner's parents refusing to meet you has nothing to do with your worth. It's not a reflection of who you are as a person. Be yourself. Act natural. SHINE.

The timing of this book is perfect and necessary as it speaks to the heart of many experiences that are often overlooked. It spoke to my personal experiences in a number of ways and touches on the very essence of humanity: our need to be accepted, to love and to be loved unconditionally. As someone who remains rejected by family for the choices I've made, this book reminds me that I am not alone. It equally gives hope to new generations as these stories are creating new legacies and traditions. I have always advocated that cultural acceptance does not mean accepting the unacceptable. These stories are a testimony to how all families are different and unique but they all have one thing in common – love. We, as a society, are richer for the relationships in this book.

Jasvinder Sanghera CBE
www.karmanirvana.org.uk
Supporting victims of honor based abuse in the United Kingdom

For so long, I have felt like I was alone in this process. That all changed when I joined the #BlindianProject. Our stories, vulnerability and values immediately created a sense of community where I've felt understood, supported and seen. This community has normalized Blindian relationships by acknowledging the trauma and loneliness we may have felt and continue to experience. I am thankful for this community for giving me the space to be 100% authentically me!

Priti Patel #BlindianProject community member

Design by SeyPEG